doodles
1 2 3

Sky Pony Press
New York

Start at point 1 and connect the dots to finish
the strands of yarn.

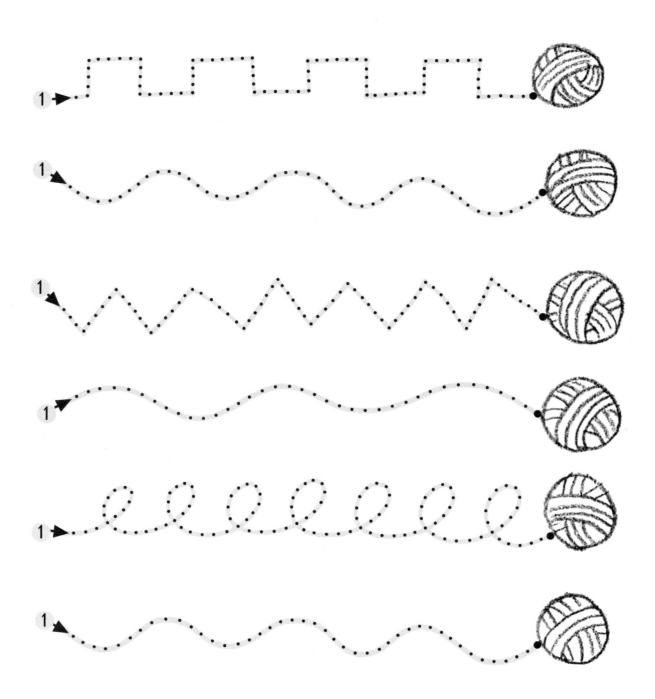

Start at point 1 and connect the dots
to cover the blanket in patterns.

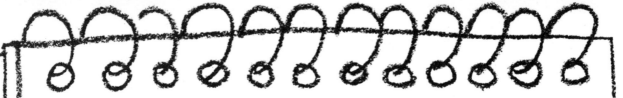

Start at point ① and connect the dots to make the numbers.

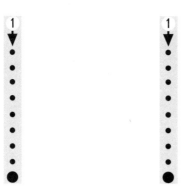

Complete and say the numbers below.

How many birds can you count?

Draw the stripes on the zebra.

Start at point **1** and connect the dots to make the numbers.

Complete and say the numbers below.

2 2 2 2 2 2 2

How many baby swans can you count?

Finish the swimming swans.

Start at point ① and connect the dots to make the numbers.

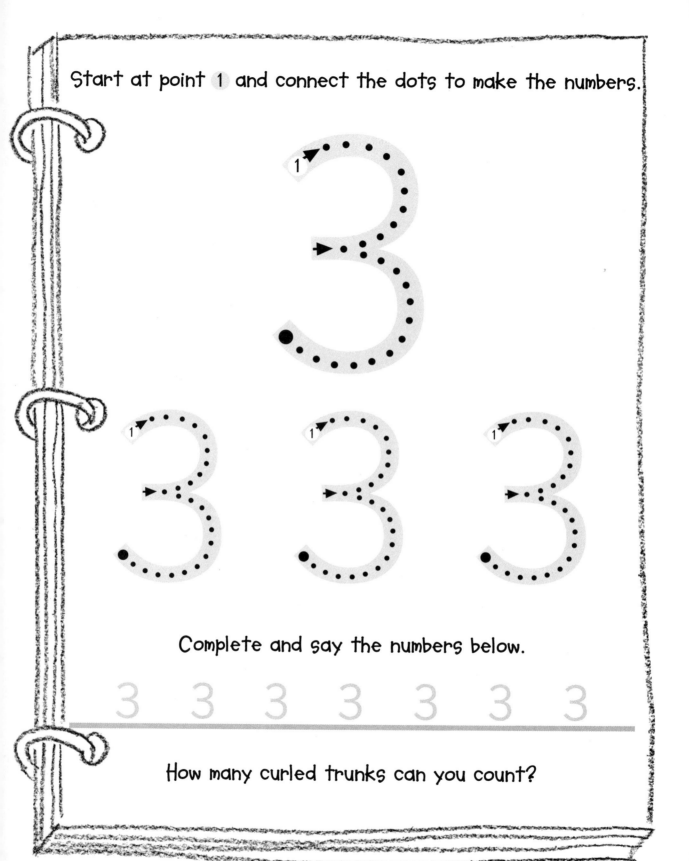

Complete and say the numbers below.

3   3   3   3   3   3   3

How many curled trunks can you count?

Draw the elephants' enormous ears.

Connect the dots from points ① and ② to make the numbers.

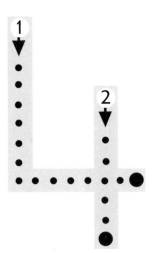

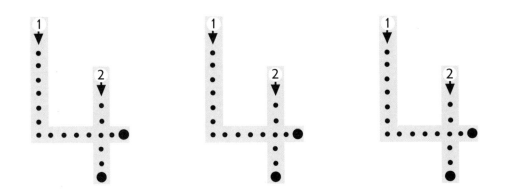

Complete and say the numbers below.

4 4 4 4 4 4 4

How many smiling people can you see?

Finish the hats on the funny people.

Connect the dots from points 1 and 2 to make the numbers.

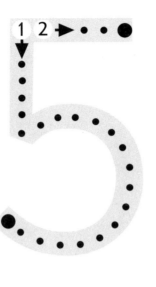

Complete and say the numbers below.

5 5 5 5 5 5 5

How many leaves can you count?

Finish the cute caterpillars.

Start at point 1 and connect the dots to make the numbers.

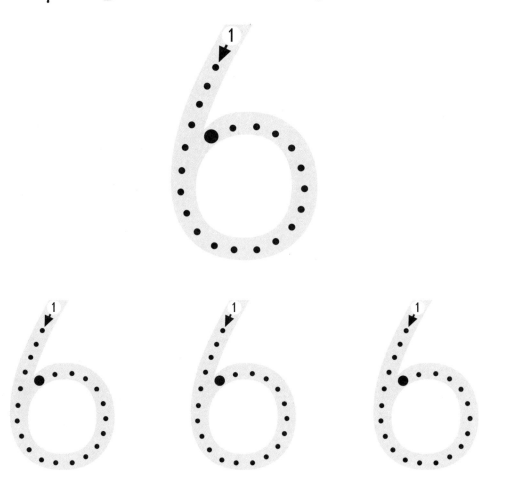

Complete and say the numbers below.

6 6 6 6 6 6 6

How many balls of yarn can you count?

Complete the cuddly kittens.

Start at point 1 and connect the dots to make the numbers.

1 ➤ • • • • •
7

1 ➤ • • • • •
7

1 ➤ • • • • •
7

1 ➤ • • • • •
7

Complete and say the numbers below.

7 7 7 7 7 7 7 7

How many seashells can you count?

Finish the super starfish.

Start at point 1 and connect the dots to make the numbers.

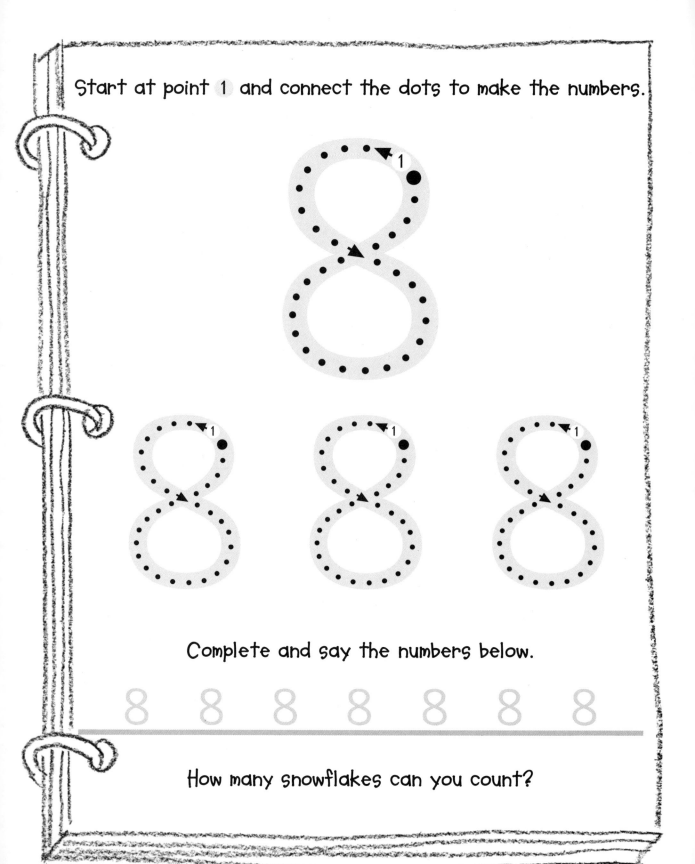

Complete and say the numbers below.

8 8 8 8 8 8 8

How many snowflakes can you count?

Complete the smiling snowmen.

Start at point **1** and connect the dots to make the numbers.

Complete and say the numbers below.

9 9 9 9 9 9 9 9

How many holes in the cheese can you count?

Finish the little mice.

Connect the dots from points ① and ② to make the numbers.

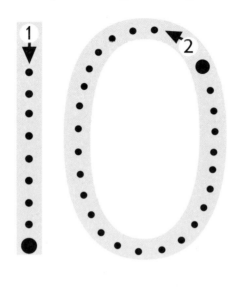

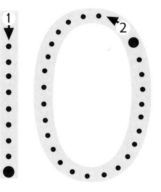

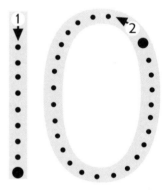

Complete and say the numbers below.

10   10   10   10   10   10   10

How many spots can you count on the ladybugs?

Finish these lovely ladybugs.

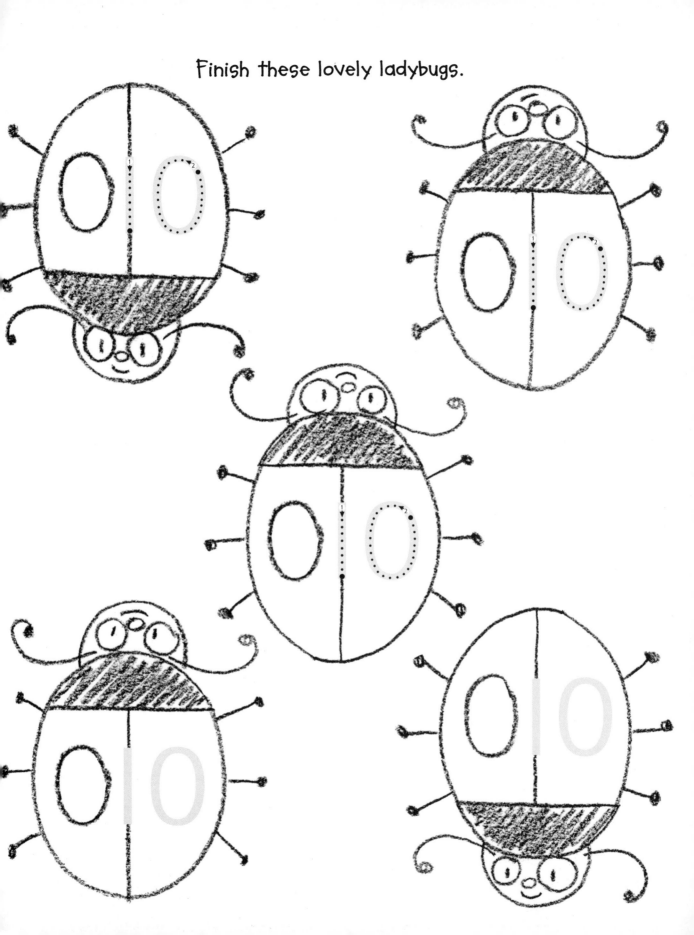

Start at point ① and connect the dots to make the numbers.

Complete and say the numbers below.

| | | | | | |

How many girls can you count?

Draw the bristles
on her toothbrush.

Start at point **1** and connect the dots to make the numbers.

Complete and say the numbers below.

2 2 2 2 2 2 2

How many hats can you count?

Finish the funny faces.

Start at point ① and connect the dots to make the numbers.

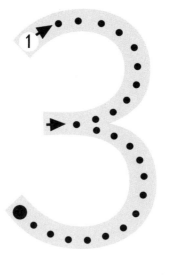

Complete and say the numbers below.

3 3 3 3 3 3 3

How many flowers can you count?

Finish the bees buzzing around the hive.

Connect the dots from points 1 and 2 to make the numbers.

Complete and say the numbers below.

4   4   4   4   4   4   4

How many reeds can you count?

Complete these fabulous flamingos.

Connect the dots from points ① and ② to make the numbers.

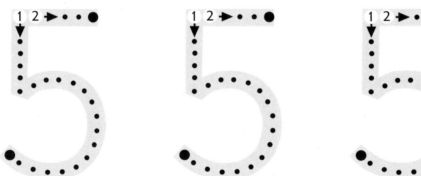

Complete and say the numbers below.

5　5　5　5　5　5　5

How many lights can you count on the spaceship?

Complete the aliens.

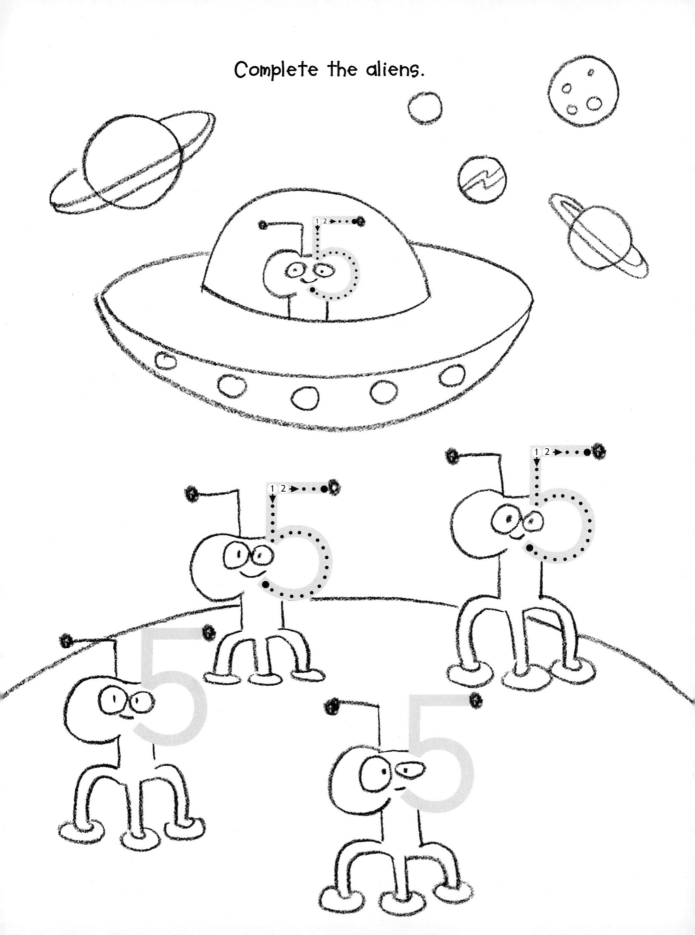

Start at point 1 and connect the dots to make the numbers.

Complete and say the numbers below.

6 6 6 6 6 6 6

How many flying feathers can you count?

Complete the beautiful birds.

Start at point 1 and connect the dots to make the numbers.

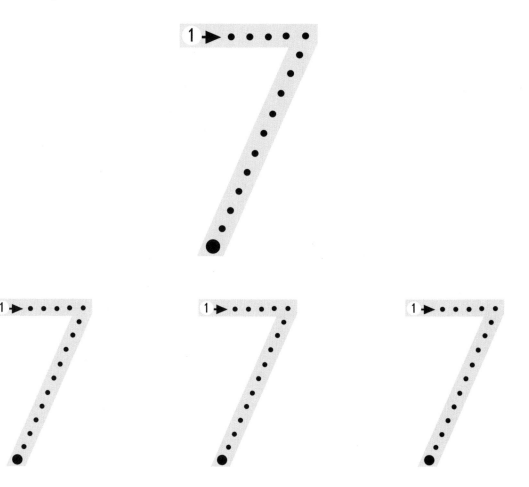

Complete and say the numbers below.

7   7   7   7   7   7   7

How many ice-cream cones can you count?

Finish the tasty ice cream.

Start at point 1 and connect the dots to make the numbers.

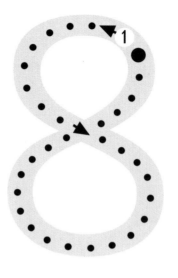

 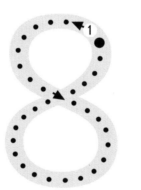 

Complete and say the numbers below.

8 8 8 8 8 8 8

How many flowers can you count?

Finish her pretty pearls.

Start at point 1 and connect the dots to make the numbers.

Complete and say the numbers below.

9 9 9 9 9 9 9 9

How many bubbles can you count?

Complete the super sea horses.

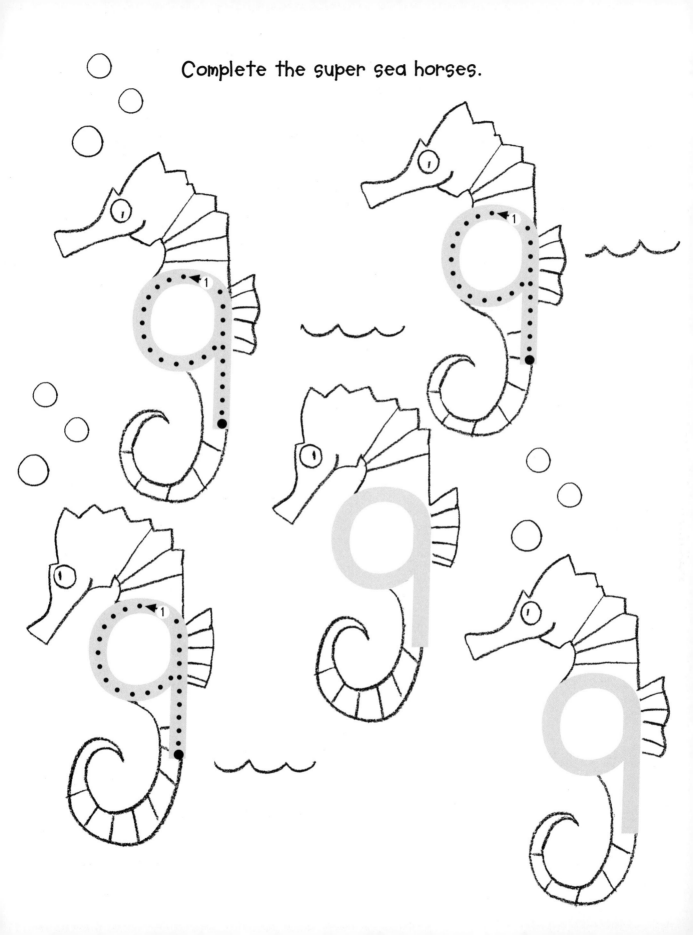

Connect the dots from points ① and ② to make the numbers.

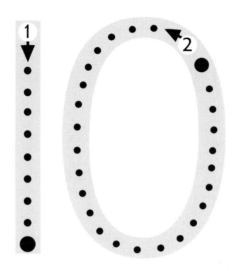

Complete and say the numbers below.

10   10   10   10   10   10   10

How many diamond shapes can you count?

Complete their sparkling crowns.

Start at point ① and connect the dots to make the numbers.

1

1   1   1

Complete and say the numbers below.

| | | | | | | |

How many pandas can you count?

Complete the bamboo for the panda.

Start at point 1 and connect the dots to make the numbers.

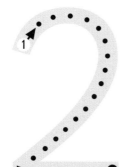  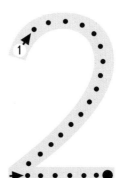

Complete and say the numbers below.

2 2 2 2 2 2 2

How many lions with manes can you count?

Complete these lovely lions' faces.

Start at point ① and connect the dots to make the numbers.

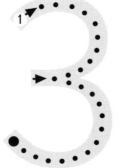

Complete and say the numbers below.

3   3   3   3   3   3   3

How many spots can you count on the dog?

Finish the dog's dreamy bones.

Connect the dots from points 1 and 2 to make the numbers.

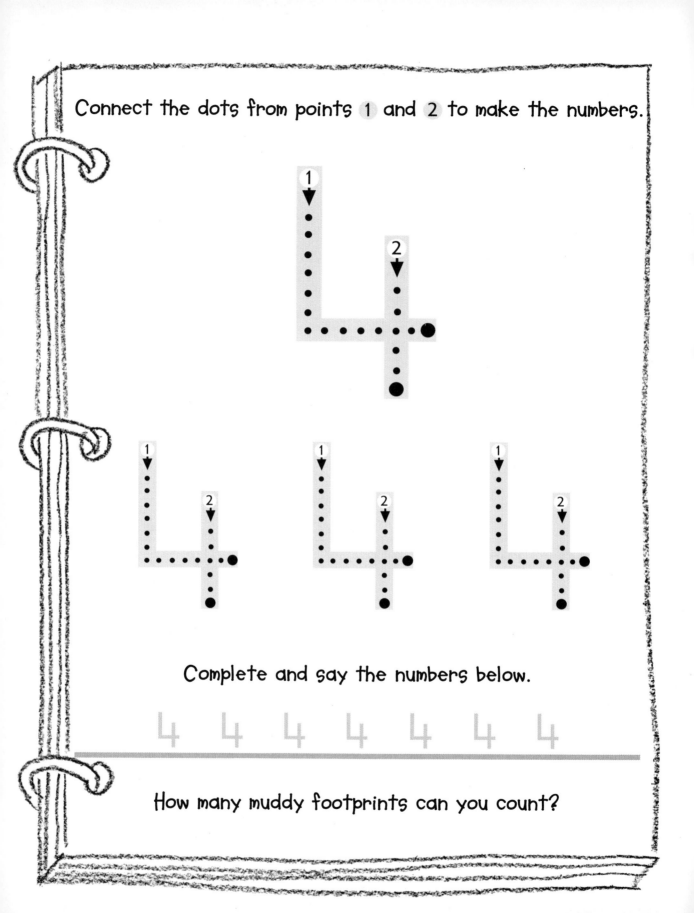

Complete and say the numbers below.

4 4 4 4 4 4 4

How many muddy footprints can you count?

Finish Fido's raincoat.

Connect the dots from points **1** and **2** to make the numbers.

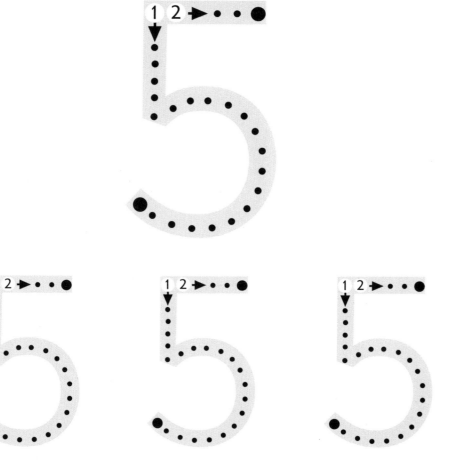

Complete and say the numbers below.

5   5   5   5   5   5   5

How many birds can you count?

Draw tasty apples in the tree.

Start at point 1 and connect the dots to make the numbers.

Complete and say the numbers below.

6 6 6 6 6 6 6

How many muddy spots can you count?

Finish the snuffling pigs' snouts.

Start at point 1 and connect the dots to make the numbers.

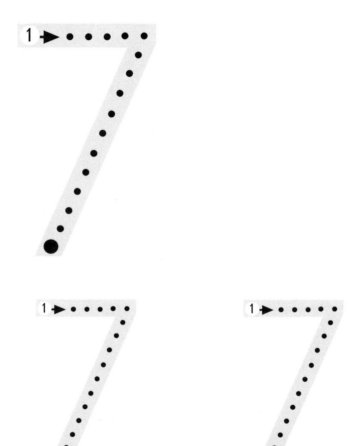

Complete and say the numbers below.

7 7 7 7 7 7 7 7

How many birds can you count sitting on the wires?

Finish the birds' beaks.

Start at point 1 and connect the dots to make the numbers.

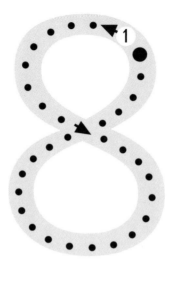

Complete and say the numbers below.

8 8 8 8 8 8 8

How many pea pods can you count?

Fill the pods
with peas.

Start at point 1 and connect the dots to make the numbers.

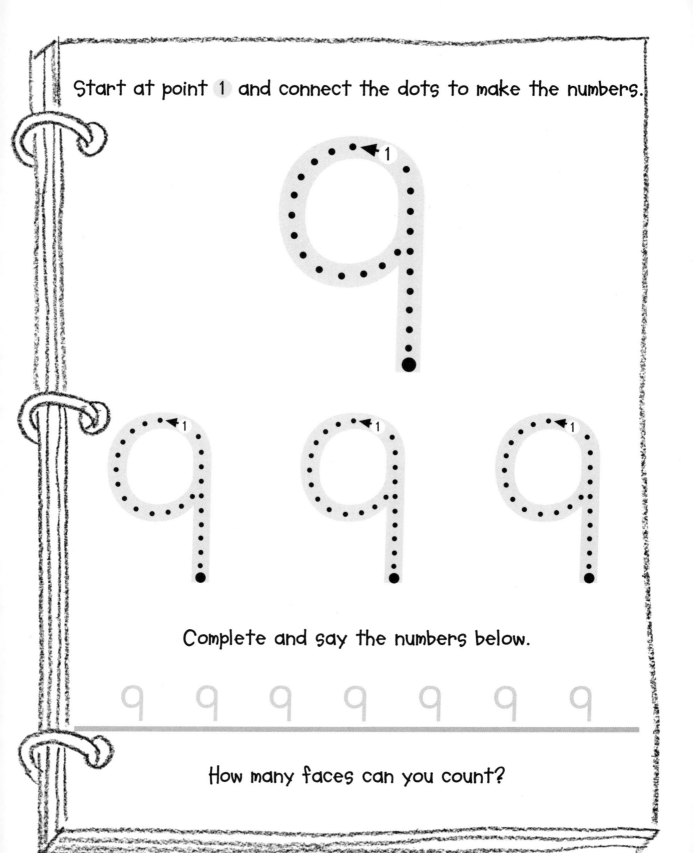

Complete and say the numbers below.

9 9 9 9 9 9 9

How many faces can you count?

Give these grownups groovy glasses.

Finish the park scene with the numbers you have learned.

It's as easy as 1, 2, 3

Teaching your child how to form his or her numbers has never been more fun! The pages at the front of this book help children to practice holding and using their pencil before tackling the numbers. Each of the pages that follow introduces a number. First, children learn to form the number by tracing the shapes provided. Then on the opposite page, they can test their skills by incorporating that number into a scene. A counting activity on each spread helps to consolidate their number knowledge.

Get a grip!

A pencil should be pinched between a child's thumb and forefinger and supported by the middle finger.

Not every child has enough strength to hold a pencil to begin with, so introduce this skill gradually to avoid discouragement.

Don't get "left" behind

Left-handers needn't feel left out. If you are left-handed and your child is right-handed, simply use your right hand when showing your child how to hold a pencil and write. If your child is left-handed and you are right-handed, use your left hand.

Written by Sally Pilkington
Illustrated by Nancy Meyers
Designed by Zoe Quayle

Sky Pony Press books may be purchased in bulk at special discounts for sales promotion, corporate gifts, fund-raising, or educational purposes. Special editions can also be created to specifications. For details, contact the Special Sales Department, Sky Pony Press, 307 West 36th Street, 11th Floor, New York, NY 10018 or info@skyhorsepublishing.com.

Sky Pony® is a registered trademark of Skyhorse Publishing, Inc.®, a Delaware corporation.

Visit our website at www.skyponypress.com.

10 9 8 7 6 5 4 3 2 1

Manufactured in China, February 2012
This product conforms to CPSIA 2008

Library of Congress Cataloging-in-Publication Data is available on file.

ISBN: 978-1-61608-664-0